SI ONLINE

timedia Resources for
TEACHERS
STUDENTS
PARENTS

SOUND PERCUSSION

MW00582368

AN INTERMEDIATE METHOD FOR INDIVIDUAL OR GROUP INSTRUCTION

Exercises for Rhythm, Meter, Rudiments, Rolls, Effects, and Performance

Dave **BLACK** | Chris **BERNOTAS**

Sound Percussion will help you on your journey to becoming a well-rounded percussionist. Here are some advantages to being proficient on more than one percussion instrument:

a. You will enhance your ability to read music, a necessary skill if you want to advance your practice, major in music at the college level, teach music, or make a living as a professional musician.

b. Playing mallet instruments and learning hand-percussion skills will increase your sensitivity to melodies, tone, and balance.

c. Ear training is critical for all musicians to develop, and playing multiple percussion instruments will help.

By using a consistent, methodical, and fun approach to presenting the concepts introduced throughout this book, we hope to promote a complete understanding of them. The well-rounded approach of *Sound Percussion* will help to give you a solid musical background and provide for the highest degree of interest and motivation. Playing percussion in an ensemble or as a soloist is also fun and will bring you many years of enjoyment. Get involved in as many musical performance groups as you can, and take advantage of any performance opportunities that come your way.

Be sure to set aside a reasonable amount of practice time on a regular basis in order to achieve the best results, and gradually work through each section of the book until you are comfortable with the materials taught.

We have made a concerted effort to present the material in an enjoyable and engaging manner, and we wish you the best of luck in becoming a part of the wonderful world of music!

SI ONLINE

Multimedia Resources for
TEACHERS
STUDENTS
PARENTS

 Audio demonstration and accompaniment tracks are included for select lines of music. Look for the audio icon throughout this book.

 Video demonstrations of exercises and key skills are included. Look for the video icon throughout this book.

 Supplemental content and additional repertoire for practice and reinforcement are available to download at the *SI Online* website below.

Visit the *SI Online* resource site to stay up to date with newly added content.
SIOnline.alfred.com

Alfred Music
P.O. Box 10003
Van Nuys, CA 91410-0003
alfred.com

ISBN-10: 1-4706-4082-1 (Book & Online Media)
ISBN-13: 978-1-4706-4082-8 (Book & Online Media)

Instrument photos courtesy of Yamaha Corporation of America Band and Orchestral Division and Sabian Cymbals
Audio and video recorded at Alfred Music Studios, Van Nuys, CA

📽 Your Instrument—The Snare Drum

THE PARTS OF THE SNARE DRUM

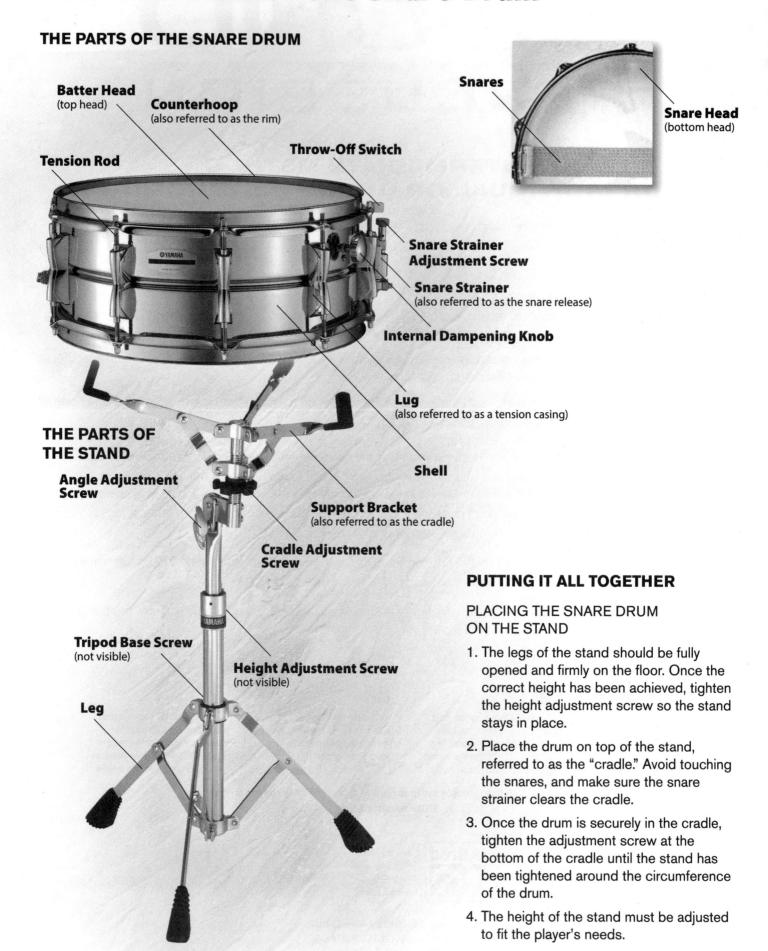

Batter Head (top head)

Counterhoop (also referred to as the rim)

Tension Rod

Throw-Off Switch

Snares

Snare Head (bottom head)

Snare Strainer Adjustment Screw

Snare Strainer (also referred to as the snare release)

Internal Dampening Knob

Lug (also referred to as a tension casing)

Shell

THE PARTS OF THE STAND

Angle Adjustment Screw

Support Bracket (also referred to as the cradle)

Cradle Adjustment Screw

Tripod Base Screw (not visible)

Height Adjustment Screw (not visible)

Leg

PUTTING IT ALL TOGETHER

PLACING THE SNARE DRUM ON THE STAND

1. The legs of the stand should be fully opened and firmly on the floor. Once the correct height has been achieved, tighten the height adjustment screw so the stand stays in place.

2. Place the drum on top of the stand, referred to as the "cradle." Avoid touching the snares, and make sure the snare strainer clears the cradle.

3. Once the drum is securely in the cradle, tighten the adjustment screw at the bottom of the cradle until the stand has been tightened around the circumference of the drum.

4. The height of the stand must be adjusted to fit the player's needs.

📽 **TUNING THE SNARE DRUM**

CHOOSING DRUMSTICKS, BRUSHES, AND MALLETS

Drumsticks are most often made of wood (usually hickory, maple, or oak). Plastic, fiberglass, and metal have been used as well, but most drummers use wood sticks, and we recommend you do as well.

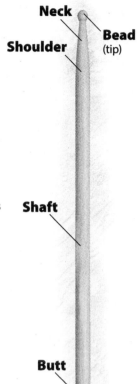

1. Drumsticks come in a variety of sizes and shapes, designed for different sounds and/or applications. A stick with a small tip is articulate, whereas one with a larger, rounder tip produces a broad, full sound.

2. Sticks are available with either a wood or nylon tip. Those with nylon tips are designed to produce a more articulate sound on the cymbals. When used on a drum, however, they sound almost identical to a wood-tipped stick.

3. "A" model sticks (originally designed for jazz playing) are smaller than "B" model sticks (designed for heavier use in jazz or concert bands), which are smaller than "S" model sticks (intended for street or marching use), which are smaller than "DC" sticks (designed for drum corps use).

4. For beginning snare drummers, we recommend a "2B" or "5B" model stick. For those playing in a jazz or concert band setting, a "5A" or "5B" drumstick is a good standard beginner stick. Whatever your choice, you should always carry multiple pairs in the event they break or get lost.

5. When purchasing sticks, check them carefully to make sure you're buying a matched pair. The following guidelines will help you make that determination:

    a. Visually inspect each stick for obvious flaws.

    b. Tap each stick on a hard surface, and listen for an even match. Sticks that produce a high pitch are most likely made of dense wood, which is excellent for both sound and response.

    c. Check to make sure the sticks are not warped by rolling each one on a hard, flat surface. Those that are warped should be set aside or discarded.

BRUSHES

Every drummer should carry at least one pair of brushes. They can be made of wire or nylon, be retractable or nonretractable, and have handles made of wood, plastic, or rubber-coated metal. Like sticks, they come in a variety of weights and styles.

MALLETS

Any of the various types of mallets covered with yarn or felt are recommended for use on the tom-toms (good for soft, muted sounds) or for suspended cymbal rolls.

HOW TO HOLD THE STICKS AND MALLETS (MATCHED GRIP)

1. First, extend your right hand as if you were going to shake hands with someone.

2. Place the stick or mallet between your thumb and the first joint of your index finger (called the **FULCRUM**), approximately a third of the way up from the butt end of the stick (*see diagram*).

3. Curve the other fingers around the stick (*see diagram*).

4. Turn your hand over so your palm is facing towards the floor (*see diagram*).

5. Repeat steps 1–4 with your left hand.

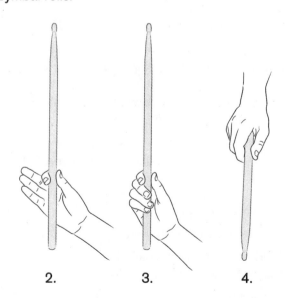

2.   3.   4.

STRIKING THE SNARE DRUM

1. Hold the tip of the right stick above the snare drum.

2. Use the wrist (not the forearm) to lift the stick about 4" off the drum.

3. Drop the stick on the drum, and let it return to the up position. It should strike near, but not on, the center of the drumhead.

4. Repeat, using the left stick.

5. Repeat, slowly, making sure both sticks strike the same beating area.

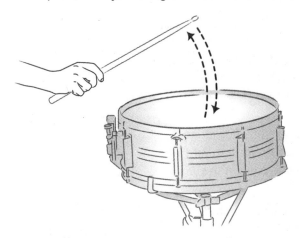

Your Instrument—The Bass Drum

The parts of the bass drum closely resemble their counterparts on the snare drum.

The bass drum is one of the largest members of the drum family. The size of the bass drum should be determined by the type of playing and by the size of the musical organization in which it is being used.

STRIKING THE BASS DRUM

1. Position the bass drum so the music stand and director can be seen in a straight line.

2. Use a soft, fairly heavy single-headed beater to strike the drum. Hold the beater in the right hand, similar to the matched grip.

3. Place the beater on the head with the thumb of the hand facing upward. Strike the head (about halfway between the center and edge of the drum) at an angle (not a direct hit), and immediately bring the beater back to its original starting position.

DAMPENING/MUFFLING THE BASS DRUM

1. To muffle the bass drum (when placed on a stationary stand), lightly touch the opposite head with the fingertips of your left hand, or by bringing the knee of your right foot into contact with the playing head. For a drum mounted to a suspended/tilted stand, lightly touch the playing head with the fingertips of your left hand.

2. The bass drum can also be muted by placing a piece of cloth over the upper head. This will produce a more subdued and less resonant sound.

CARE AND MAINTENANCE

1. Drumheads may be cleaned with a damp cloth or mild soap and water.

2. Metal shells and hoops may be cleaned with a damp cloth and/or metal polish. Wood and pearl finishes can be cleaned with a damp cloth and mild soap.

3. Tension rods should be lubricated with white lithium grease.

4. A stick bag is recommended for the storage and transportation of your sticks, mallets, and brushes. They come in a variety of sizes, styles, colors, and materials.

Note: When using cleaning supplies, teacher supervision is strongly recommended.

Sound Notation

Music has its own language and symbols that are recognized worldwide.

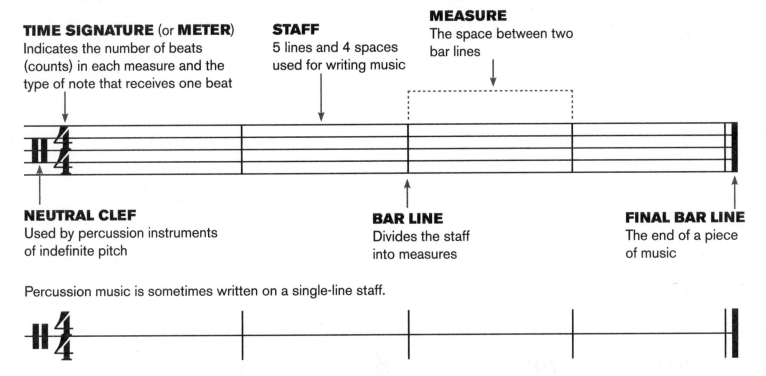

TIME SIGNATURE (or **METER**)
Indicates the number of beats (counts) in each measure and the type of note that receives one beat

STAFF
5 lines and 4 spaces used for writing music

MEASURE
The space between two bar lines

NEUTRAL CLEF
Used by percussion instruments of indefinite pitch

BAR LINE
Divides the staff into measures

FINAL BAR LINE
The end of a piece of music

Percussion music is sometimes written on a single-line staff.

Traditional noteheads are used for membrane (snare drum, bass drum), pitched wood and non-pitched wood instruments. Alternate noteheads |✕ ◇ △| may be used for metallic instruments.

RHYTHM TREE

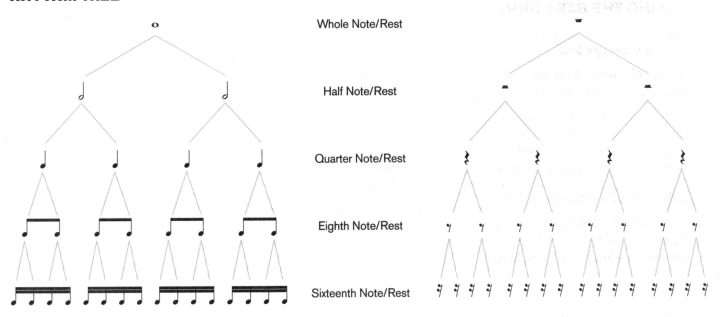

Whole Note/Rest

Half Note/Rest

Quarter Note/Rest

Eighth Note/Rest

Sixteenth Note/Rest

An **ARTICULATION** indicates the way a note should be played. An **ACCENT** (>) is an articulation that tells you the note should be played with a stronger attack.

STACCATO (·) is an articulation or style of playing that is light and separated. It is indicated with a dot. The staccato articulation can be used at slower tempos where the attack or sustain of a note can be better controlled. At a slower tempo, play the note half its normal length. Although staccato articulation is not common in percussion music, all musicians should understand this concept.

DYNAMICS

ppp   **PIANISSISSIMO**—very, very soft

pp   **PIANISSIMO**—very soft

p   **PIANO**—soft

mp   **MEZZO PIANO**—medium soft

mf   **MEZZO FORTE**—medium loud

f   **FORTE**—loud

ff   **FORTISSIMO**—very loud

fff   **FORTISSISSIMO**—very, very loud

cresc. and ‹——   **CRESCENDO**—gradually play louder

decresc. and ——›   **DECRESCENDO OR DIMINUENDO**—gradually play softer

HOW TO PRACTICE

As you play through this book, some parts will be very easy while others may require more time to play well. Practicing your instrument every day will help you achieve excellence. Carefully play each exercise until you can perform it comfortably three times in succession.

▶ Practice in a quiet place where you can concentrate.

▶ Schedule a regular practice time every day.

▶ Remember to maintain good posture and hand position.

▶ Start each practice session with the basic drum rudiments (special sticking combinations for snare drum). Practice each one open (slow) to closed (fast) to open (slow).

▶ Focus on the music that is most difficult to play, then move on to the music that is less challenging.

Sound Rhythm: Level 1
Quarter Notes through Whole Notes in 𝄴

SOUND CONCEPTS

Due to the slow decrease in sound of the bass drum, **DAMPENING** may be necessary (see page 4 for more information). Sometimes there will be an indication to **LET RING** (notated with either l.v. or a half tie ⌣). When you see this, do not dampen the drum.

SOUND ADVICE:

▶ Practice the exercises in Level 1 within the tempo range of ♩ = 80–132 until you can play each one comfortably. Be sure to count! Play each of the exercises at a medium volume level.

▶ Throughout the book, you may notice some rhythms that look different but sound the same (exercise 6, measures 1 and 2). A well-rounded percussionist must be able to interpret various ways rhythms can be written.

8

SOUND REINFORCEMENTS

SOUND ADVICE:

▶ Remember to dampen/muffle on the rests.

▶ Exercise 18 contains a one-bar repeat. It means to repeat the music of the previous measure.

SOUND ADVICE: Remember to dampen on the rests.

SOUND COMBINATIONS

* Icons with an asterisk indicate that the media has only mallet and timpani.

Sound Rhythm: Level 2
Eighth Notes, Dotted Quarter Notes, and Syncopation in $\frac{4}{4}$
SOUND CONCEPTS

SOUND ADVICE: Each exercise in this section has a repeat. Feel free to repeat any exercise as needed.

12

SOUND ADVICE:

▶ Notice the repeat with first and second endings in exercises 59 and 63. Follow the roadmap when you see markings like these.

▶ Exercises 60–64 are extra reinforcement for the dotted quarter note. Be sure to keep a steady stream of eighth notes in mind while you play. This is an important skill called subdividing.

14

SYNCOPATION occurs when there is emphasis on a weak beat.

SOUND ADVICE:

▶ There are many syncopated rhythms reinforced on this page. Be sure to keep a steady subdivision.

▶ Remember: Some rhythms look different but sound the same.

SOUND REINFORCEMENTS

16

SOUND COMBINATIONS

Sound Rhythm: Level 3
Sixteenth Notes in 4/4

SOUND CONCEPTS

SOUND ADVICE:

▶ While the Sound Concept exercises are written in unison, the bass drum part has been simplified throughout this book to maintain rhythmic clarity.

▶ For exercises 98–115 you may choose to repeat them to make eight-measure phrases, if desired.

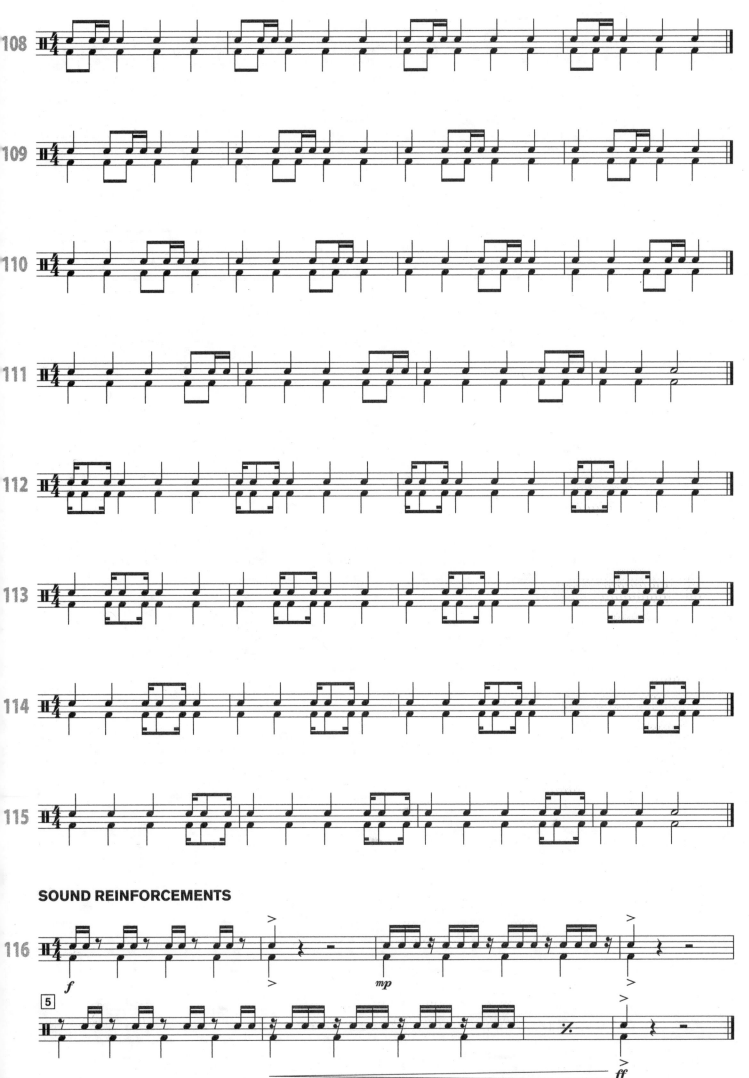

SOUND REINFORCEMENTS

20

SOUND COMBINATIONS

Sound Rhythm: Level 4
Sixteenth Notes with Dots and Ties in 4/4

SOUND CONCEPTS

24

SOUND REINFORCEMENTS

SOUND COMBINATIONS

A **TIE** is a curved line that connects two or more notes. The tied notes are played as one longer note with the combined value of both notes.

SOUND REINFORCEMENTS: TIES

SOUND COMBINATIONS

SOUND ADVICE: When your part is marked with Solo, the marked section is meant to be brought out as a highlight of the music.

Sound Rhythm: Level 5
Triplets in 4/4

SOUND CONCEPTS

SOUND REINFORCEMENTS

SOUND COMBINATIONS

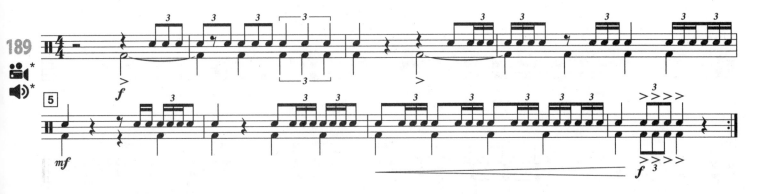

SOUND ADVICE: For exercises such as 187, be sure to consider the complexity of the rhythms when choosing a tempo.

32

Sound Meter: Level 1
Simple Duple Meters

SOUND CONCEPT: 2/4 METER

194

SOUND REINFORCEMENT

195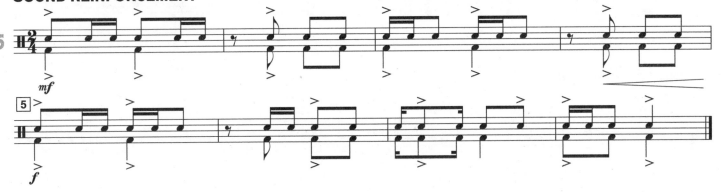

SOUND COMBINATION

196

SOUND CONCEPT: 3/4 METER

197

SOUND REINFORCEMENT

198

SOUND COMBINATION

Measure one of the exercise below incorporates what is refered to as a **HEMIOLA**. A hemiola is a rhythm where the grouping of accents gives the effect of a shift in meter. The first measure of exercise 199 creates the feeling of two beats per measure rather than three.

199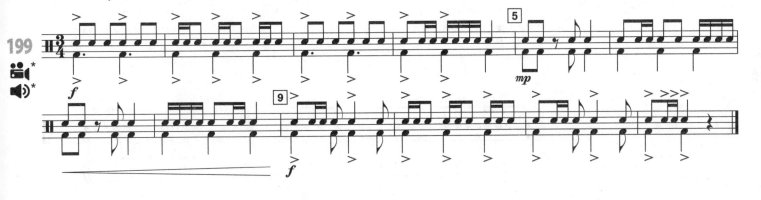

34

SOUND CONCEPT: $\frac{5}{4}$ METER

200

SOUND REINFORCEMENT

201

SOUND COMBINATION

202

SOUND CONCEPT: $\frac{6}{4}$ METER

203

SOUND REINFORCEMENT

204

SOUND COMBINATION

205

SOUND CONCEPT: CUT TIME (¢) OR 2/2 METER

SOUND REINFORCEMENTS

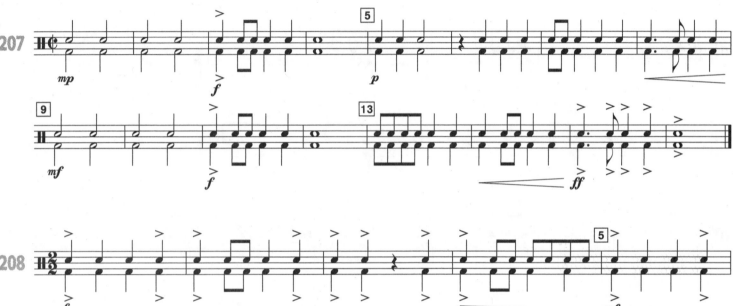

SOUND COMBINATION

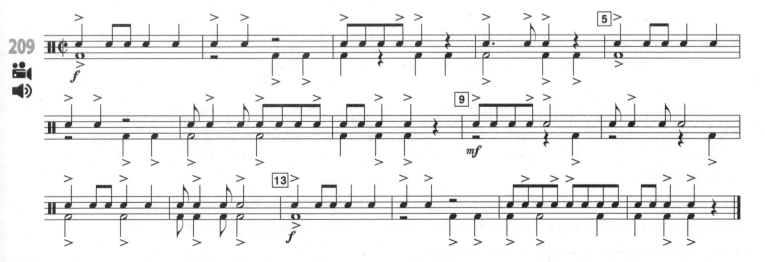

Sound Meter: Level 2
Compound Meter ($\frac{6}{8}$)

SOUND CONCEPTS

SOUND ADVICE:

▶ Exercises in $\frac{6}{8}$ should be practiced with two dotted-quarter-note beats per measure and with six eighth-note beats.

▶ Exercise 210 contains a two-bar repeat. It means to repeat the music of the previous two measures.

▶ Notice the similarity in sound between exercises 217 and 218.

SOUND ADVICE: Notice the similarity in sound between exercises 220 and 221.

SOUND COMBINATIONS

Sound Meter: Level 3
Compound Meter ($\frac{6}{8}$ Sixteenths and Dots)

SOUND CONCEPTS

SOUND REINFORCEMENTS

SOUND COMBINATIONS

Sound Meter: Level 4

$\frac{3}{8}$, $\frac{9}{8}$, and $\frac{12}{8}$

SOUND CONCEPT: $\frac{3}{8}$ METER

250

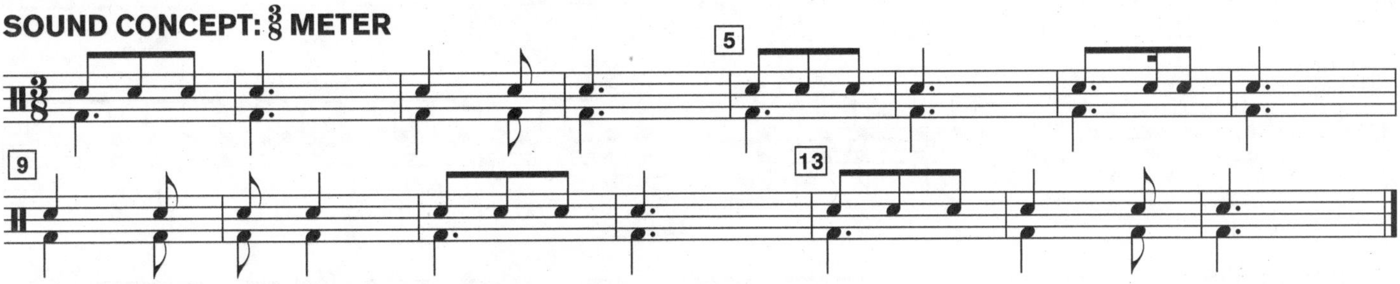

SOUND REINFORCEMENT

251

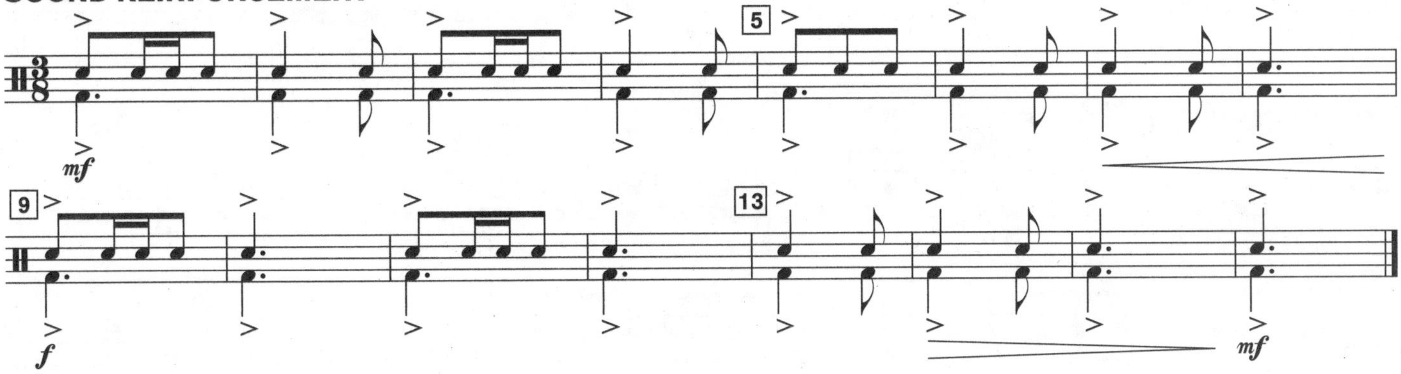

SOUND COMBINATION

252

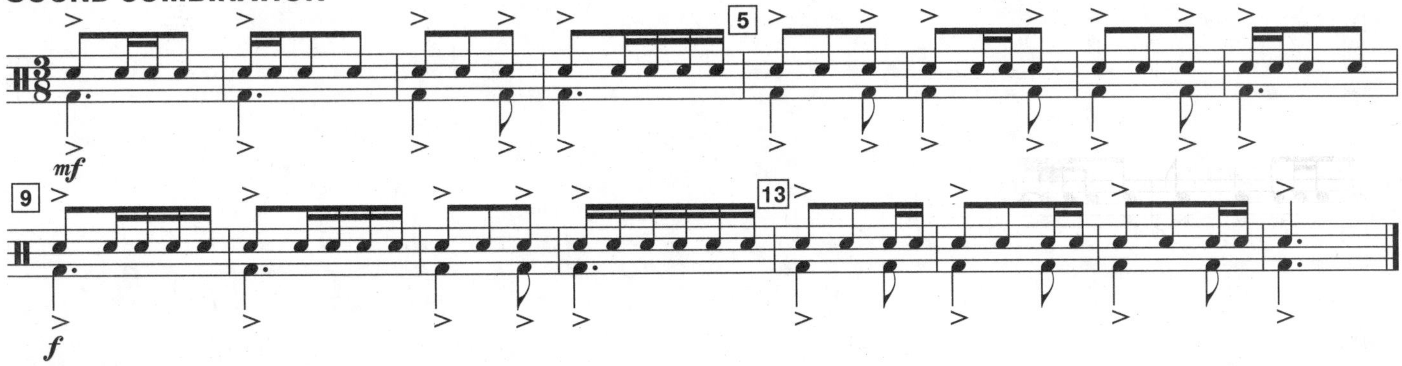

SOUND CONCEPT: $\frac{9}{8}$ METER

253

SOUND REINFORCEMENT

254

SOUND ADVICE: $\frac{3}{8}$ should be practiced with three eighth-note beats per measure and with one dotted-quarter-note beat per measure.

44

SOUND COMBINATION

255

SOUND CONCEPT: 12/8 METER

256

SOUND REINFORCEMENT

257

SOUND COMBINATION

258

Sound Meter: Level 5
Asymmetrical Meter

Whereas most meters have a consistent beat, in asymmetrical meters the beat is uneven. These are expressed as beats that subdivide into two and beats that subdvide into three. In the following exercises, keeping a steady eighth-note subidvision in mind will help keep the meter accurate.

SOUND CONCEPT: $\frac{5}{8}$ METER (2+3)

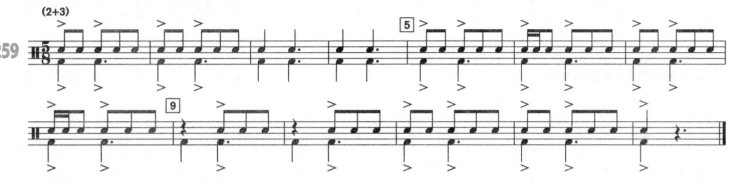

SOUND REINFORCEMENT

SOUND CONCEPT: $\frac{5}{8}$ METER (3+2)

SOUND REINFORCEMENT

46

SOUND CONCEPT: $\frac{7}{8}$ METER (2+2+3)

SOUND REINFORCEMENT

SOUND CONCEPT: $\frac{7}{8}$ METER (3+2+2)

SOUND REINFORCEMENT

SOUND CONCEPT: ⅞ METER (2+3+2)

(2+3+2)

SOUND REINFORCEMENT

(2+3+2)

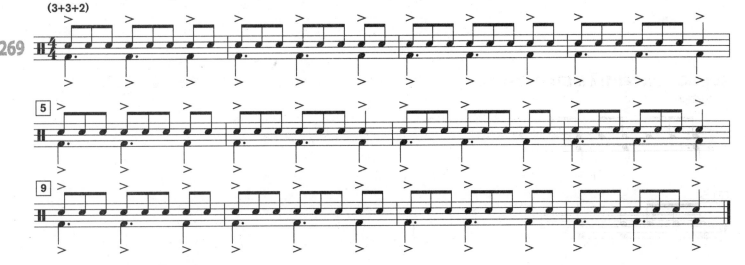

SOUND CONCEPT: 4/4 METER (3+3+2)

(3+3+2)

SOUND REINFORCEMENT

(3+3+2)

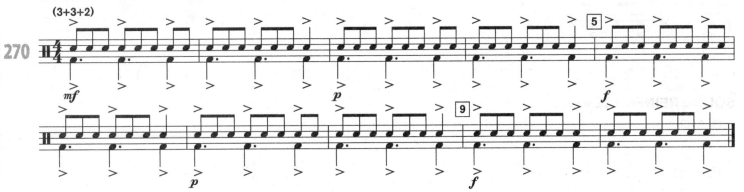

SOUND CONCEPT: 4/4 METER (2+3+3)

(2+3+3)

SOUND ADVICE: Exercises 269–272 show how a common time, such as 4/4, can be used as a complex or asymmetrical meter.

48

SOUND REINFORCEMENT

SOUND COMBINATIONS: ASYMMETRICAL METERS

SOUND ADVICE: When there are multiple measures repeated, like in exercise 275, sometimes you will see a number above the repeat to help you keep track of where you are in the music.

Sound Meter: Level 6
Changing Meter
SOUND CONCEPT: $\frac{3}{4}$ TO $\frac{6}{8}$

SOUND CONCEPT: $\frac{4}{4}$ TO $\frac{3}{4}$

281

SOUND CONCEPT: $\frac{6}{8}$ TO $\frac{7}{8}$

282

SOUND CONCEPT: $\frac{5}{8}$ TO $\frac{7}{8}$

283

Fun Fact

In 1933 at the American Legion National Convention in Chicago, drummers from around the country met to discuss methods of drumming and drum instruction. This group of thirteen gentlemen selected thirteen rudiments they believed all drummers should know. These "Essential 13" rudiments were used as a test for membership in the Thirteen Club, organized for the promotion of rudimental drumming by the National Association of Rudimental Drummers (N.A.R.D.). In later years, thirteen additional rudiments were combined with the original thirteen to form the **STANDARD 26 AMERICAN DRUM RUDIMENTS**.

Sound Rudiments: Level 1
Diddles

SOUND CONCEPT

The **SINGLE PARADIDDLE** is a combination of two single strokes and one group of double strokes, with an accent on the first note. Example: RLRR LRLL

SOUND REINFORCEMENTS

52

SOUND COMBINATIONS

288

289

SOUND CONCEPTS

The **DOUBLE PARADIDDLE** consists of two sets of single strokes and one group of double strokes, with an accent on the first note. Example: RLRLRR LRLRLL

290

291

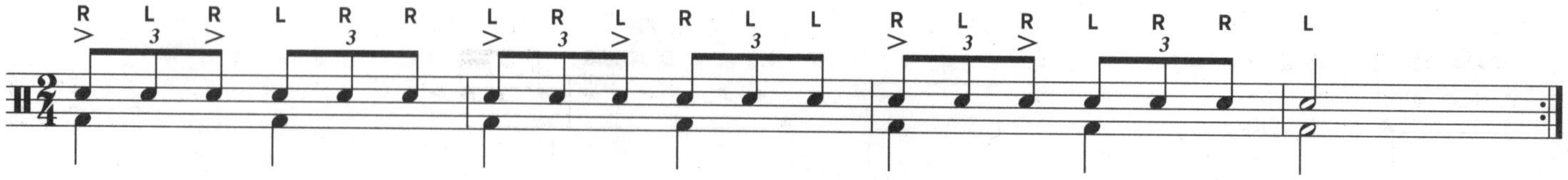

53

SOUND REINFORCEMENTS

SOUND COMBINATIONS

Sound Rudiments: Level 2
Flams/Grace Notes

SOUND CONCEPT

📹 The **FLAM** is a combination of a small note (grace note) and a main note. To play a flam, position one stick close to the drumhead (2" to 3") and one stick above the drumhead (8" to 10"). Bring both sticks down at the same speed. For instruments other than a snare drum, flams are called **GRACE NOTES** and can be performed in a similar way with various sticking patterns depending on the what makes the most musical sense.

SOUND REINFORCEMENT

SOUND CONCEPT

📹 The **FLAM ACCENT** combines a flam with two other single strokes. They are played alternately.

SOUND REINFORCEMENT

SOUND CONCEPT

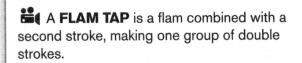

A **FLAM TAP** is a flam combined with a second stroke, making one group of double strokes.

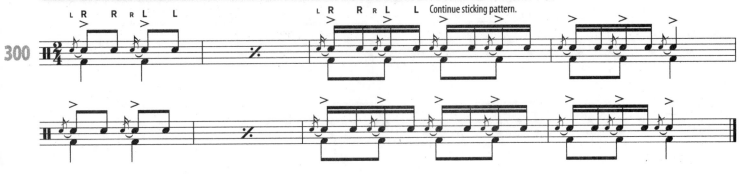

SOUND REINFORCEMENT

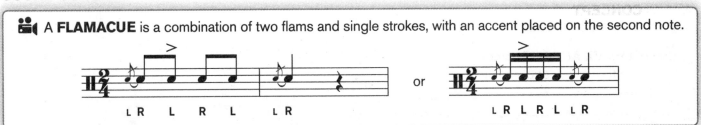

SOUND CONCEPT

A **FLAMACUE** is a combination of two flams and single strokes, with an accent placed on the second note.

SOUND REINFORCEMENT

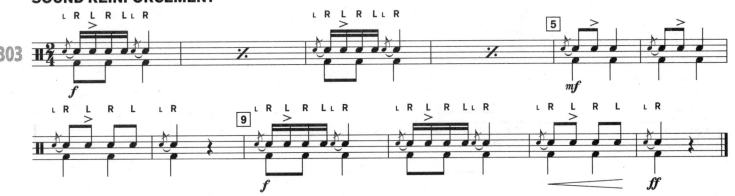

56

SOUND CONCEPT

The **FLAM PARADIDDLE** combines a flam with a single stroke and one group of double strokes.

SOUND REINFORCEMENT

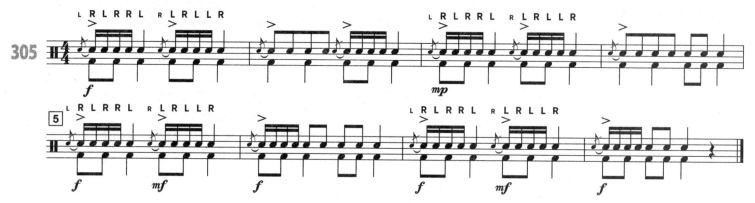

SOUND COMBINATION: FLAMS

Sound Rudiments: Level 3

Drags

SOUND CONCEPT

The **DRAG** (or **THREE-STROKE RUFF**) consists of two small notes (grace notes) and a main note. The two grace notes are played softer than the main note. The drag may begin with either hand.

SOUND REINFORCEMENT

SOUND CONCEPT

The **DRAG PARADIDDLE #1** is formed by a tap, followed by two small notes (grace notes) in front of a single paradiddle.

SOUND REINFORCEMENT

58

SOUND CONCEPT

The **SINGLE RATAMACUE** is a combination of a drag followed by three single strokes, usually ending with an accent.

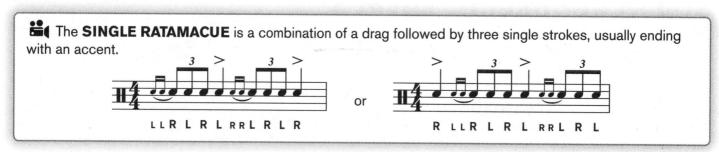

SOUND REINFORCEMENT

SOUND CONCEPT

The **FOUR-STROKE RUFF** consists of three small notes (grace notes) and a main note. The rudiment is played with single strokes, and may begin with either hand.

Continue simlar sticking.

SOUND REINFORCEMENT

SOUND COMBINATIONS

Sound Rolls: Level 1
Single-Stroke Roll

To execute a **SINGLE-STROKE ROLL**, alternate the sticks (R-L and L-R) and make sure you maintain an even sound and speed. Practice slowly at first with a metronome. Gradually increase your speed, and continue to listen to the quality of the sound and consistency of the strokes. Rolls on the *bass drum* are most often achieved using single strokes produced with two mallets. See the diagram of the mallet grip on page 77.

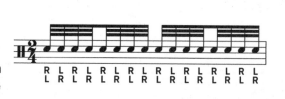

Multiple-Bounce Roll (also referred to as a "Buzz" or Unmeasured Roll)

A **MULTIPLE-BOUNCE/BUZZ ROLL** is an unmeasured roll comprised of multiple bounces on each stick. It can be notated either with a diagonal line or with a "*z*" (most often found in marching band music).

In order to achieve a clear, clean, and connected **MULTIPLE-BOUNCE/BUZZ ROLL**, drop each stick onto the drumhead, and let them bounce back naturally (slightly increasing the pressure between the thumb and first knuckle to control the bounces). Experiment with how you strike the drum, as well as the pressure between your thumb/first fingers, so the multiple bounces are compressed into a smooth, singular buzz sound. Do not squeeze the back three fingers tightly around the sticks, as too much pressure will reduce the number of bounces each stroke produces. Those fingers should make light contact with each stick and be used to help maintain control of the stick's motion. This skill will take some experimentation and practice in order to accomplish the desired, seamless sound. Use active listening to be sure the sound of both hands is the same.

EXERCISE 1

Strike the drum with either the right or left hand, starting the stroke from about 5" to 6" above the drumhead. Allow the stick to bounce. Use your ear (as a wind player would to tune his or her instrument) to find the right amount of pressure, as well as the best area of the drumhead, to produce a good sound.

Play the following exercises without a metronome and unmetered.

EXERCISE 2

EXERCISE 3

Once you are able to produce a good, clear sound with many bounces per hand, overlap the sound from one hand to the next, keeping a connected "buzz."

SOUND ADVICE: Use critical thinking to achieve the best sound possible—listen, evaluate, and adjust!

SOUND CONCEPT: MULTIPLE-BOUNCE ROLL/CHROMATIC SCALE

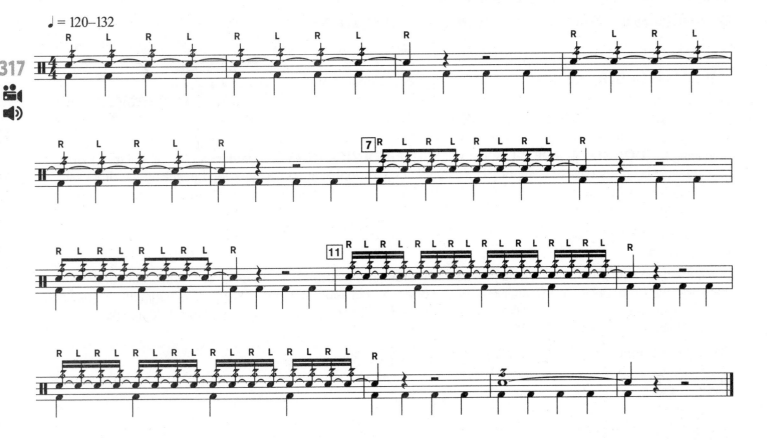

Fun Fact

With the goal of standardizing, revising, and updating the Standard 26 American Drum Rudiments, the Percussive Arts Society (PAS) introduced the PAS International Drum Rudiments, using the Standard 26 American Drum Rudiments as their nucleus. Added to the traditional 26 rudiments are 14 drum corps, orchestral, European, and contemporary drum rudiments, forming what is now referred to as the **PAS 40 INTERNATIONAL DRUM RUDIMENTS**.

Sound Rolls: Level 2
Double-Stroke Roll (also referred to as an Open Roll)

The **DOUBLE-STROKE ROLL** is a series of connected double strokes.

In order to produce a clean, clear double-stroke (or open) roll, you will need to build control of the bounce by practicing the **DOUBLE STROKE**. Like the **MULTIPLE-BOUNCE ROLL**, the double-stroke roll will take plenty of practice in order to achieve a smooth, consistent sound. A double stroke is achieved by striking the drum with enough downward pressure to start the bounce, but *lifting* the stick after the second bounce to ensure an even sound of both strikes.

EXERCISE 1

Strike the drum with the right or left hand repeatedly, starting the stroke from about 5" to 6" above the drumhead. Allow the stick to bounce, and *lift* after the second bounce. Use your listening skills as you experiment to make sure *both* strikes make an even sound. Also experiment to find the best area of the drumhead to produce what you think is a good sound.

Play the following exercise without a metronome, and unmetered.

EXERCISE 2

Once you are able to achieve a consistent sound from both strikes, with both hands, begin working with a metronome, and continue developing a controlled, even stroke and sound.

EXERCISE 3

Connect the strokes from one hand to the other. Do not forget to practice starting with your non-dominant hand. You can start with a slow tempo and gradually increase the speed.

Open Rolls vs. Closed Rolls

When playing closed or open rolls your hands will play the same subdivision. Open rolls have a specific number of bounces, closed rolls have an unspecific number of bounces. Exercises on the following pages that use open rolls should also be practiced with closed rolls by moving the hands in the same subdivision but with buzz strokes instead of double strokes.

Open

Closed

SOUND ADVICE: Use critical thinking to achieve the best sound possible—listen, evaluate, and adjust!

SOUND CONCEPT: OPEN ROLL/CHROMATIC SCALE

Sound Rolls: Level 3
Roll Rudiments

SOUND REINFORCEMENT

SOUND CONCEPT: 17-STROKE ROLL

SOUND REINFORCEMENT

SOUND CONCEPT: 7-STROKE ROLL

SOUND REINFORCEMENT

SOUND ADVICE:

▶ The 7-stroke roll appears in this order because of the difficulty of the roll and the fact that it is not alternated the way the 5- and 9-stroke rolls are.

▶ Practice all rolls in this section as closed/buzz and open/double strokes.

SOUND COMBINATIONS

68

Sound Rolls: Level 4

Triplet Roll and Rudiments

SOUND CONCEPT

There is a consistent triplet pulse throughout this exercise to encourage a steady pulse through the subdivision. The slashes indicate double strokes.

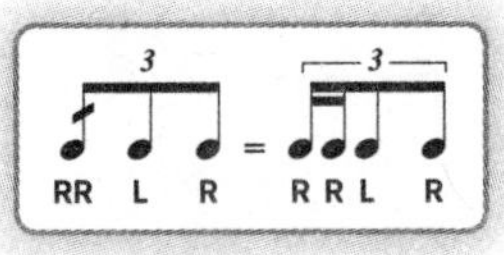

338

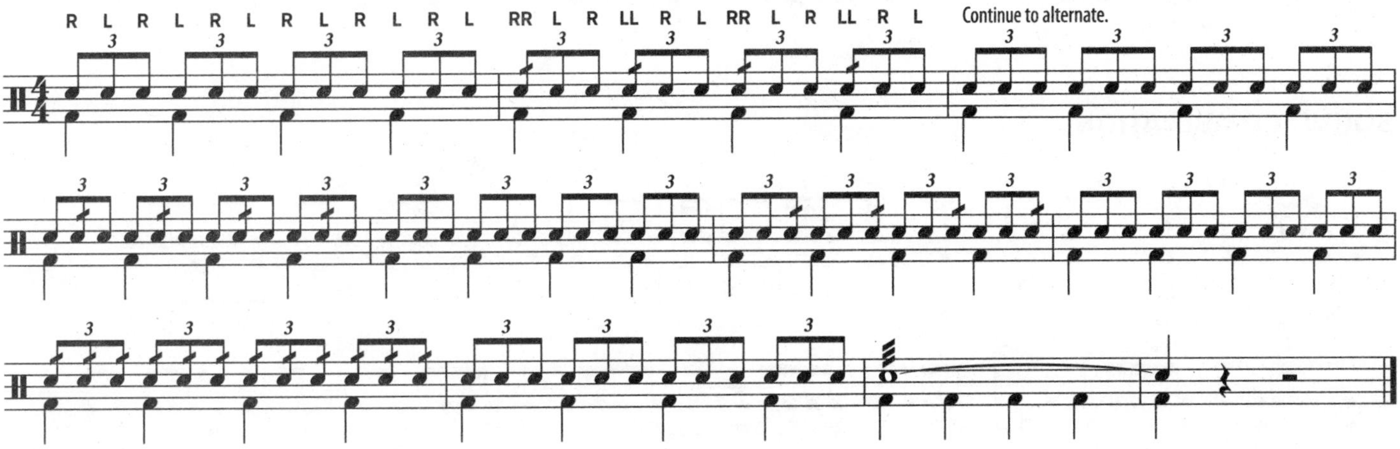

SOUND CONCEPT: 7-STROKE ROLL (TRIPLET)

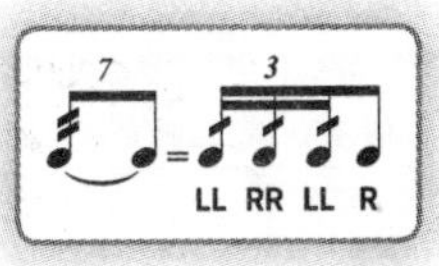

339

SOUND REINFORCEMENT

340

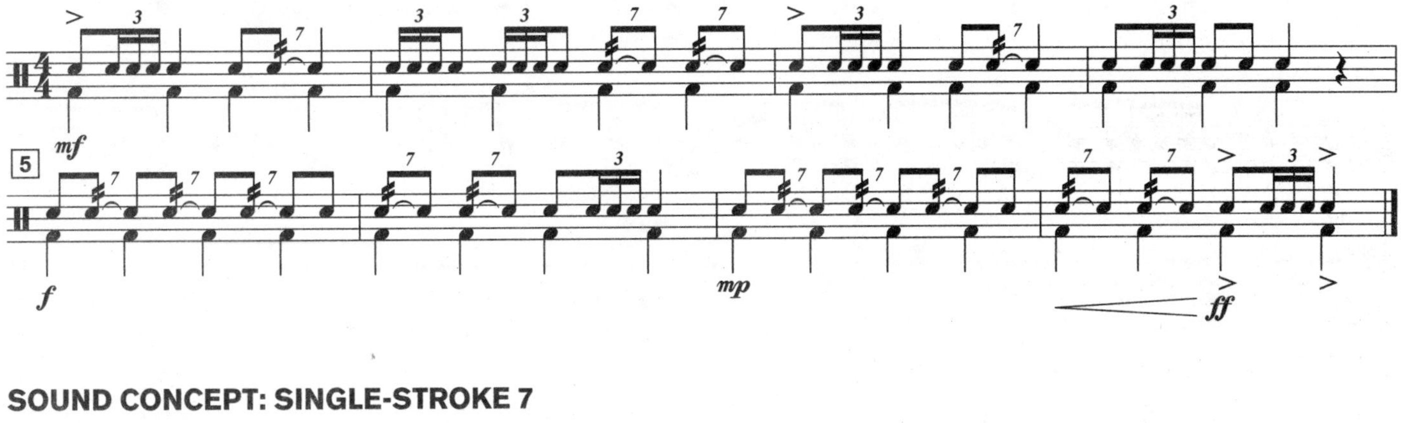

SOUND CONCEPT: SINGLE-STROKE 7

341

70

SOUND REINFORCEMENT

342

SOUND COMBINATION

343

TRIPLET ROLL (COMPOUND METER)

344

Sound Rolls: Level 5
Rolls in Compound Meter

Rolls in compound meter are treated differently if the eighth-note beat is felt or if the dotted-quarter-note beat is felt. Here is a guide.

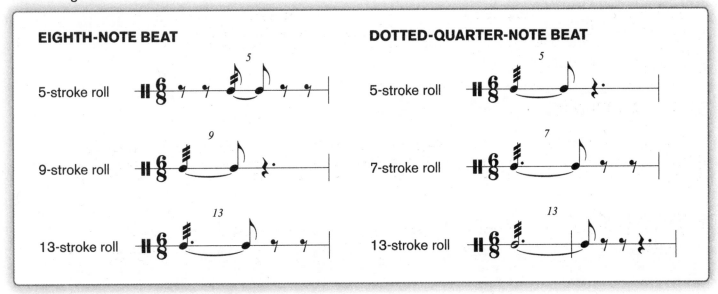

SOUND CONCEPT: 5-STROKE ROLL (EIGHTH-NOTE BEAT)

345

SOUND REINFORCEMENT

346

SOUND CONCEPT: 9-STROKE ROLL (EIGHTH-NOTE BEAT)

347

SOUND REINFORCEMENT

348

SOUND ADVICE: The stroke number is not always included, therefore you (and your teacher) will have to make appropriate decisions regarding stroke count.

72

SOUND CONCEPT: 13-STROKE ROLL (EIGHTH-NOTE BEAT)

349

SOUND REINFORCEMENT

350

SOUND CONCEPT: 5-STROKE ROLL IN 2

351

SOUND REINFORCEMENT

352

SOUND CONCEPT: 7-STROKE ROLL IN 2

353

SOUND REINFORCEMENT

354

SOUND CONCEPT: 13-STROKE ROLL IN 2

355

SOUND REINFORCEMENT

SOUND COMBINATIONS

SOUND ADVICE: Exercises 357–360 can be performed in six or in two. Use the appropriate roll for the tempo.

74

Sound Rolls: Level 6
Duple and Triplet Roll Application

In triplet rolls, the hands play a triplet subdivision rather than a duple subdivision. The use of a triplet roll versus that of a duple depends on the tempo of the music. As a general rule, if the pulse or beat is too fast to successfully achieve a clear roll with a duple subdivision, then a triplet roll should be used. For example, if the quarter-note pulse is 180 BPM, that would require the use of an eighth-note-triplet roll. If the quarter-note pulse is 90 BPM, a sixteenth-note-sextuplet roll would be required.

Since a well-executed roll maintains a continuous and even sound, the listener will most likely not know which subdivision is being used, and so the end result will be a musically satisfying roll. It will be up to you (and your teacher) to determine which roll subdivision will be the most appropriate. For the following exercises, it is important to practice at the indicated tempo in order for the triplet and duple rolls to be effective.

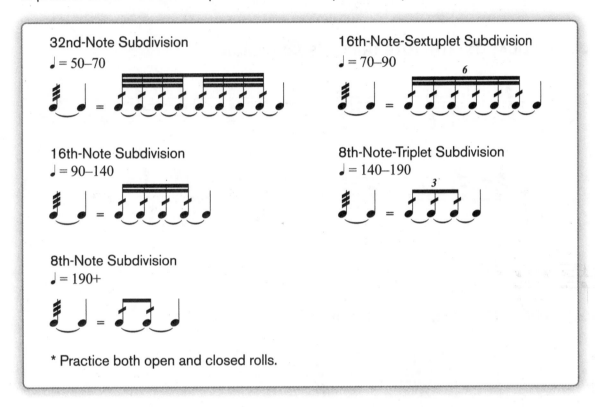

DUPLE/TRIPLET ROLL APPLICATION: 32ND-NOTE SUBDIVISION

DUPLE/TRIPLET ROLL APPLICATION: 16TH-NOTE-SEXTUPLET SUBDIVISION

DUPLE/TRIPLET ROLL APPLICATION: 16TH-NOTE SUBDIVISION

DUPLE/TRIPLET ROLL APPLICATION: 8TH-NOTE-TRIPLET SUBDIVISION

DUPLE/TRIPLET ROLL APPLICATION: 8TH-NOTE SUBDIVISION

🎥 Sound Effects

SNARE DRUM

- To produce a **stick shot** (S.S.), place the tip of one stick on the drumhead, and strike it in the middle with the other stick. Stick shots are usually notated with an "×" notehead.

- A pistol-shot effect can be produced with a **rim shot** (R.S.). A rim shot is produced by striking the head and rim simultaneously with a drumstick. Rim shots are usually notated with an "×" notehead.

- By disengaging the snares (with the lever on the side of the drum), the snare drum can serve as a substitute **tom-tom**. Specify "snares off" on the part.

- To play on the rim, strike the rim on the far side of the drum with the shoulder or shaft of the stick. This is usually notated with an "×" notehead.

- A stick click is produced by hitting one stick against the other using both butt ends, a butt end and a tip, or both tips.

- To produce a **cross-stick** sound, hold the opposite end of the stick, leave the tip of the stick resting on the drumhead, lift the butt end of the stick, and strike the rim of the drum. Cross-sticks are usually notated with either an "×" or an "⊗" with a circle notehead.

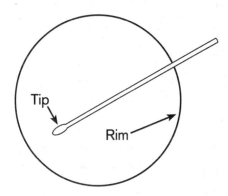

BASS DRUM

- A soft roll can produce a faintly threatening sound much like that of **distant thunder**.

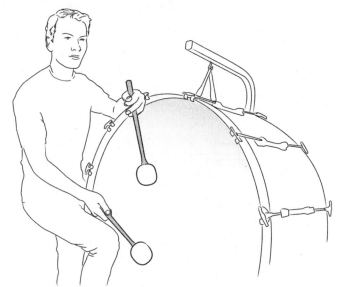

- An explosive **canon-shot effect** can be achieved by forcefully striking the drum dead center.

- The bass drum may be played with **timpani or marimba mallets** for more active and involved rhythmic figures.

- To create a unique rubbing sound effect, pull a **superball mallet** across the surface of a bass drum head.

- To produce a different or **more contrasting tone**, you can play the drum with your fingers, or use a different type of beater in each hand. Specify "play with fingers or beater" on the part.

Sound Performance

THE STARS AND STRIPES FOREVER

J. P. Sousa

ENGAGE

Glossary

1st and 2nd endings – Play the 1st ending the first time through; repeat the music, but skip over the 1st ending on the repeat, and play the 2nd ending instead.

accent (>) – Play the note with a strong attack.

articulation – Indicates how a note should be played.

attack – The manner in which a sound begins.

balance – Occurs when performers adjust their volume so all players in the ensemble can be heard.

batter head – The playing side of any drum.

bead (or *tip*) – The end of the drumstick normally used to strike the drum or cymbal.

bearing edge – The outside circumference of the drum, where the head meets the shell.

brushes – Devices made of wire or nylon, used to strike or sweep a drumhead or cymbal.

butt end – The end opposite the tip of a drumstick.

buzz roll – Comprised of multiple bounces with each stick and used to sustain the sound of the drum.

cases – Used to store and/or transport drums, cymbals, and accessories.

choke – To strike the bass drum, crash cymbals or suspended cymbal, and then dampen it immediately.

counterhoop (or *rim*) – Used to apply tension and hold the drumhead in place.

cradle – The top part of a snare stand that holds a drum.

crescendo – Gradually play louder.

crisp sound – Sharp, clean, and clear.

dampening (*muffling*) – Used to stop the bass drum, triangle, suspended cymbal, or crash cymbals from ringing.

decay – The gradual fading out of a sound.

decrescendo or diminuendo – Gradually play softer.

dot – Increases the length of a note by half its value.

double bar line – Indicates the end of a section.

double paradiddle – A combination of two sets of single strokes and one group of double strokes, with an accent on the first znote.

double stroke – Play two strokes with each hand.

double-stroke roll (also referred to as an *open roll*) – Comprised of a series of connected double strokes.

drag (or *three-stroke ruff*) – A combination of two small notes (grace notes) and a main note.

drag paradiddle #1 – A combination of a tap, followed by two small notes (grace notes) in front of a single paradiddle.

drumhead – The material (plastic or skin) stretched over one or both ends of a drum and struck with a hand, mallet, or stick.

drum key – A key used to tighten or loosen the tension rods for the purpose of tuning or removing drumheads.

drumstick – A stick used to strike a drum or cymbal, consisting of a tip (or bead), shoulder, shaft, and butt end.

duple roll – Uses a duple subdivision under the roll.

dynamics – Varying degrees of volume.

finger dampening – To stop a tone from resonating, gently touch the instrument with your fingers.

five-stroke roll – A series of two double strokes, followed by a single stroke (RRLLR or LLRRL).

flam – A combination of a small note (grace note) and a main note.

flamacue – A combination of two flams and single strokes, with an accent placed on the second note.

flam accent – Combines a flam with two other single strokes.

flam paradiddle – Combines a flam with a single stroke and one group of double strokes.

flam tap – A flam combined with a second stroke, making one group of double strokes.

forte (f) – Play loudly.

fortissimo (ff) – Play very loudly.

fortississimo (fff) – Play very, very loudly.

half-tie (let-ring tie) ($\smile$) – Let vibrate until the sound dies away.

harmonic overtones – High pitches, other than the fundamental pitch, that resonate after a drum or cymbal has been struck.

internal dampening knob – Mounted on the outside of the shell and attached to the internal muffler; when turned clockwise, the muffler presses against the batter head.

internal muffler – When pressed against the batter head, it absorbs some of the vibrations and eliminates the after-ring or resonance.

laissez vibrer (l.v.) – Let vibrate until the sound dies away.

largo – A slow tempo.

let ring – Let vibrate until the sound dies away.

lugs – Attached to the side of the drum and used as receptacles for the tension rods.

mallets – Sticks with a yarn- or felt-covered ball at the end, used to strike a drum or keyboard mallet instrument, or to produce suspended cymbal rolls.

matched grip – Both hands hold a drumstick or mallet in the same manner (generally, with palms down).

mezzo forte (mf) – Medium loud.

mezzo piano (mp) – Medium soft.

moderato – A medium tempo.

muffle or muffler – A device used to absorb vibrations and eliminate after-ring.

muffling – A technique used to reduce head resonance, ring, or harmonic overtones.

multiple-bounce roll – Comprised of multiple bounces with each stick and used to sustain the sound of the drum.

muted – Softened or muffled.

neutral clef – Used by percussion instruments of indefinite pitch.

nine-stroke roll – A series of four double strokes, followed by a single stroke (RRLLRRLLR or LLRRLLRRL).

octave – The interval of an eighth.

one-measure repeat ($\%$) – Play the previous measure again.

opaque drumhead – A nontransparent drumhead.

open roll (also referred to as a *double-stroke roll*) – Comprised of a series of connected double strokes.

piano (p) – Play softly.

pickup note – Occurs before the first complete measure of a phrase.

phrase – A musical statement or idea.

rallentando – Becoming gradually slower.

rehearsal mark – Reference number or letter in a box above the staff.

repeat sign – Go back to the beginning or repeat sign, and play the music again.

resonance – A ringing or long decay.

right-facing repeat – Indicates where to begin repeating the music.

rim (or *counterhoop*) – Used to hold a drumhead in place.

rim shot – Produced by simultaneously hitting the rim and head of the drum with a drumstick.

ring – A resonant tone.

ritardando – Becoming gradually slower.

rolls – Use rapid, alternating strokes beginning with either hand.

rudiments – Special sticking combinations for snare drum.

seven-stroke roll – A series of three double strokes, followed by a single stroke (LLRRLLR).

seventeen-stroke roll – A series of eight double strokes, followed by a single stroke (RRLLRRLLRRLLRRLLR or LLRRLLRRLLRRLLRRL).

shaft – The middle part of a drumstick between the shoulder and the butt end.

shell – The frame that supports all the other components of the drum.

shoulder – The area of a drumstick between the tip (bead) and the shaft.

single paradiddle – A combination of two single strokes and one group of double strokes, with an accent on the first note.

single-stroke roll – Comprised of alternating single strokes (R–L and L–R).

single ratamacue – A combination of a drag followed by three single strokes, usually ending with an accent.

snare head – The bottom head of a snare drum.

snare release (or *snare strainer*) – Attached to the side of the snare drum, used to engage or disengage the snares from the snare head by means of a throw-off switch.

snares – Wire, nylon, cable, or gut strands stretched across the outside surface of the snare head.

snare strainer – See *snare release*.

solo – When one person is performing alone or with accompaniment.

staccato (·) – An articulation or style of playing that is light and separated.

stick bag – Used for the storage and transportation of sticks, brushes, and mallets.

stick shot – Produced by placing the tip of one stick on the drumhead and striking it in the middle with the other stick. Also known as a stick-on-stick shot.

style marking – Sometimes used instead of a tempo marking to help musicians understand the feeling the composer would like the music to convey.

syncopation – Occurs when there is emphasis on a weak beat.

tacet – To be silent (do not play a movement or section).

tempo markings – Indicate the speed of the music.

tension adjustment knob – Used to adjust the tension or pressure of the snares.

tension rod – Used to hold the counterhoops in place and adjust the tension of the drumhead.

thirteen-stroke roll – A series of six double strokes, followed by a single stroke (RRLLRRLLRRLLR or LLRRLLRRLLRRL).

throw-off switch – Used to engage or disengage the snares from the head.

tie – A curved line that connects two or more notes on the same line or space; the tied notes are played as one longer note with the combined value of both notes.

timbre – Tone color or quality.

time signature or meter – Indicates the number of beats (counts) in each measure and the type of note that receives one beat.

tip (or *bead*) – The end of the drumstick normally used to strike the drum or cymbal.

tone control knob – Mounted on the outside of the shell of the snare drum (and some tom-toms) and attached to the internal muffler; when turned clockwise, the muffler presses against the batter head.

triplet roll – Uses a triplet subdivision under the roll.

tuning – Changing or adjusting an instrument to sound at a specific pitch.

two-measure repeat ($\overset{2}{/\!\!/}$) – Repeat the two previous measures.